GOD MADE ME FOR HEAVEN

Helping Children Live for an Eternity with Jesus

Marty Machowski

**Illustrated by
Trish Mahoney**

Then I saw a new heaven and a new earth, for the first heaven and the first earth had passed away, and the sea was no more. And I saw the holy city, new Jerusalem, coming down out of heaven from God, prepared as a bride adorned for her husband. And I heard a loud voice from the throne saying, "Behold, the dwelling place of God is with man. He will dwell with them, and they will be his people, and God himself will be with them as their God. He will wipe away every tear from their eyes, and death shall be no more, neither shall there be mourning, nor crying, nor pain anymore, for the former things have passed away."

Revelation 21:1-4

Dear Parent or Caregiver,

I wrote this book to help you pass on the truth about heaven to your children. Popular culture teaches that heaven is a place far up in the sky where people with wings like angels' float among the clouds singing hymns and playing music on golden harps.

The Bible describes heaven very differently. Sure, Jesus did ascend into the clouds when he left to be with his Father in heaven, but he promised he would come back again and live with us here on a re-created earth. One day the trumpet will sound and Jesus will return. He'll put an end to all sin, sickness, and sorrow and live among his children on a new earth—a new garden of Eden—where everything will be made new. Imagine what it will be like to enjoy mountains and valleys, the sky and the seas, and explore them all with Jesus. Heaven was meant to be a new paradise on earth.

I hope that this book will help to replace any fear of death with hope for heaven, love for Jesus, and a longing for his return. Imagine if someone told you that you've been granted eternal life and you never have to die. Instead, one day you'll wake up to a new reality in a world where everyone is kind to one another, no one ever gets sick, and nothing ever goes wrong. This is exactly what Jesus promises everyone who believes in him. Jesus said, "I am the resurrection and the life. Whoever believes in me, though he die, yet shall he live, and everyone who lives and believes in me shall never die. Do you believe this?" (John 11:25-26).

May God bless you and your family through these pages.

By God's grace,
Marty Machowski

As Leo gulped down the last bite of his breakfast, he heard a knock at the back door.

"They're here!" he shouted.

It was the best day of the year—the first day of summer vacation!

"Can I go out and play?" Leo asked.

"Summer break is the best!"
Leo said as he high-fived Tiana,
David, Roxy, Emma, and Jaden.
The sun shone bright and warm, and the
swallows dipped and dove through the air.
They were glad it was summer too!

"No more homework,"
David cheered.

"No getting up early,"
Jaden added.

"We get to play all day!"
Roxy said.

To the castle!

Leo shouted, leading his friends over the rope bridge.

The bridge led to a huge playhouse. Leo's Grandpa Joe finished building the castle three years ago, just before he went to heaven. The castle had a tower, a ladder, a slide, and a fire pole.

Leo's grandmother greeted the children. "Good morning," she said and waved.

Leo slid down the fire pole and gave her a big hug.

"Sure is a beautiful day," Grandma said. "A good time to plant flowers. Grandpa always loved the orange ones best. They reminded him of a warm summer sunrise."

"Do you miss Grandpa?"
Leo asked.

"I sure do.
We planted the flowers together
every year until he got sick.
Now he's with Jesus in heaven,
just where he always wanted to be."

"Does he have wings like an angel?"
Roxy asked as she slid down the slide with her hands in the air.

"No, Roxy, only angels have wings," Grandma told her. "When Grandpa Joe died, only his spirit went to be with Jesus in heaven. His body went back to the dust.

Grandpa Joe is waiting for the day when Jesus will return to earth and make all things new and give him a brand-new, glorious body—bright as the sun.

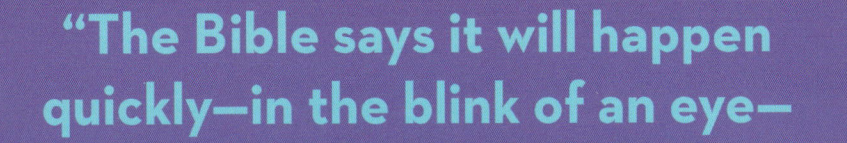

"The Bible says it will happen quickly—in the blink of an eye—

when the last trumpet sounds.

And when that happens, those who have died will be raised to live forever. Then Jesus will transform our bodies to be like his glorious body."*

*1 Corinthians 15:52; Philippians 3:21

"When Grandpa went to heaven, he left his sickness, sorrow, and sin deep in the grave.

Now Grandpa Joe is singing and dancing and praising in heaven!"
Grandma danced in her flower garden.

"We were made for heaven, and I can't wait till I get there too!"

"Heaven sounds boring—
aren't we just singing all the time?"
Tiana asked.

"Boring? No way!"
Grandma answered.

**"Think of heaven like a
summer vacation that never ends!**

When you woke up this morning to the sunshine,
you all raced to come out here and play all day.
That's what heaven will be like.

"Every day, I pray God's trumpet will sound for the Lord to return. This time he'll come with his sword.

Jesus will put an end to the curse of sin, suffering, sickness, and death," Grandma told them.

"I thought Jesus was like a gentle lamb. I didn't know he has a sword," David said.

"Jesus came as a Lamb to die in our place on the cross, and then he rose from the dead. Jesus took our punishment so we could be forgiven. And because Jesus rose from the dead, we can be sure that all who believe in him will also be resurrected!" Grandma explained.

"When Jesus returns, he's coming back as **the Lion of Judah.** He will save everyone who believes in Jesus and throw Satan and death and all his evil followers into the lake of fire."

"I hope I'm good enough to be saved and go to heaven," Leo said.

"How good do you have to be?" Leo started thinking about how just this morning he had been mean to his sister.

"No one's good enough,"

Grandma answered.
"That's why we need Jesus.

"Jesus lived a perfect life. He always obeyed and never sinned. Now Jesus offers to trade **his goodness** for **our sin.** Jesus will give everyone who trusts in him credit for his perfect life. All we have to do is turn from our sin and believe in Jesus."

"Do you remember the thief on the cross?" Grandma asked.

"Who was he?" Tiana asked.

"Let me tell you the story," Grandma said.

That was his way of asking Jesus to forgive him for his sins. Jesus answered, **'Truly, I say to you, today you will be with me in paradise.'"***

"Is the thief praising Jesus with Grandpa?" Leo asked.

"He sure is," Grandma answered.

*Luke 23:42-43

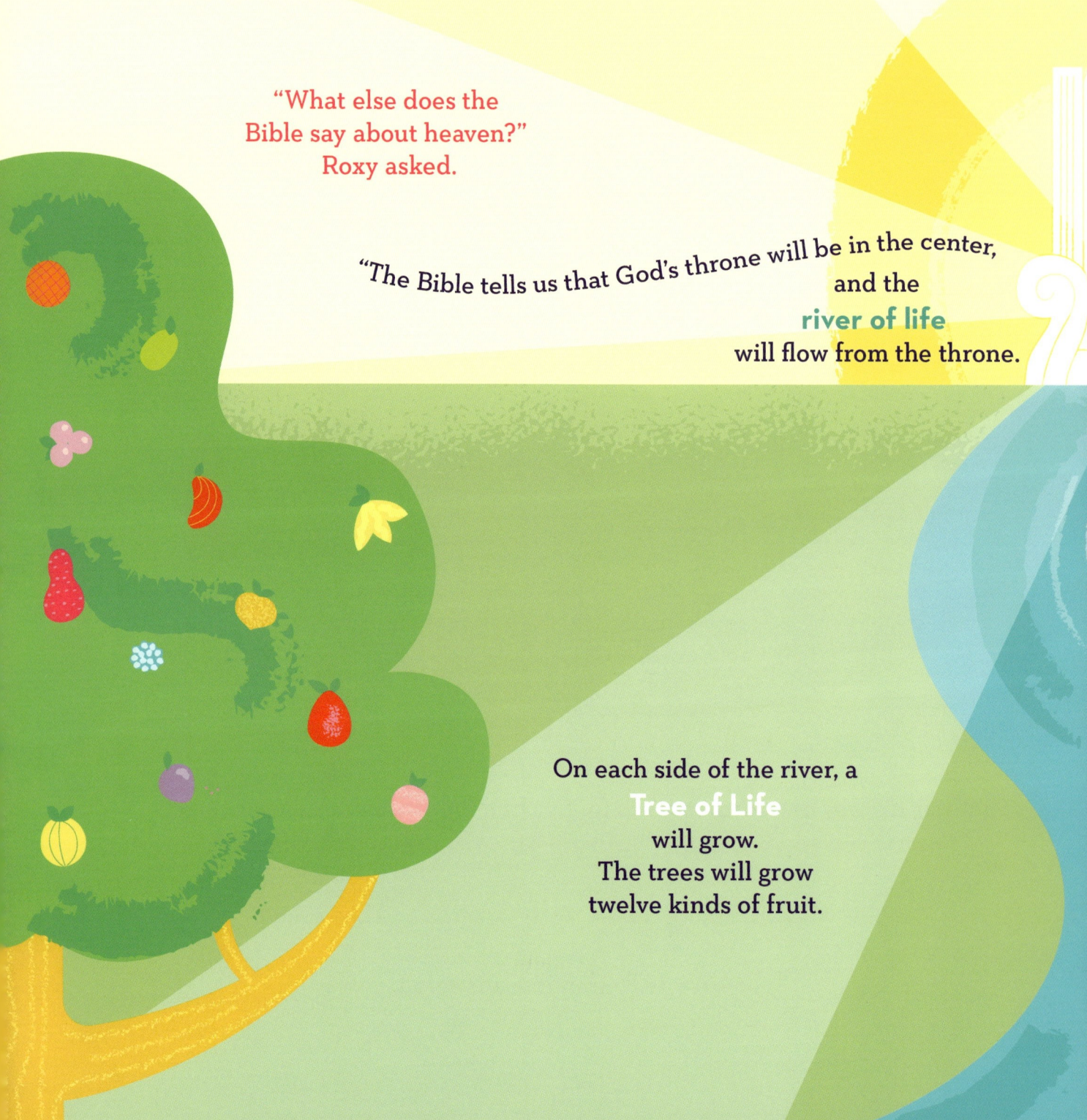

"What else does the Bible say about heaven?" Roxy asked.

"The Bible tells us that God's throne will be in the center, and the **river of life** will flow from the throne.

On each side of the river, a **Tree of Life** will grow. The trees will grow twelve kinds of fruit.

We won't have any need for lightbulbs or sunshine because the glory shining from Jesus will light up the whole world— even brighter than the sun."*

"Wow, that sounds amazing!" Roxy shouted.
"I love fruit. It's my favorite thing to eat!"

*Revelation 11:1–5

"When Jesus returns and destroys all evil, all God's children will gather around his throne. There will be people from every tribe and nation shouting,

**WORTHY IS THE LAMB!*

It will be one great party."

*Revelation 5:12

"Like a summer vacation that never ends!"
Leo shouted.

Grandma held up a flower.

"Every summer, I plant these flowers, and every fall they die. But one day, I'll plant flowers in the new heavens and new earth that will never die. The flowers I plant will go on growing forever, and so will I."

"I'll bet Grandpa will help you again," Leo said.

"Oh yes, I'm sure he will," Grandma said with a smile.

Looking over toward the house, she said, "We were not made for a world of death and sin. We were made for heaven. That is why we must believe and trust in Jesus.

God made me for heaven.
And God made you for heaven too.

"How about we celebrate the beginning of your summer vacation with a party that reminds us of what we have to look forward to in heaven someday? It looks like your mom has already set one up for you."

All the children yelled,

"Hurray!"

and ran off to where Leo's mom was setting up an end-of-the-school-year party.

"Look," said Roxy, "Your mom has strawberries, raspberries, bananas, and watermelon for us to eat. I wonder what twelve fruits will grow on the Tree of Life in heaven."

"I bet the fruit in heaven is better than anything we have ever tasted here," said Tiana as she filled her mouth with strawberries.

"Yes," agreed Grandma. "Good food, great friends, and even summer vacation are a small taste of heaven. But these earthly things all come to an end.

The joys of heaven—living with Jesus and joining in his victory party—will last forever."

Teaching Children about HEAVEN

Talking about heaven with your children is always a great way to spend your time. As you talk, make sure that you are using the Bible—that will keep your conversation on the right track. You can look up the Bible verses listed here and also use the discussion questions to guide your conversation.

Where is heaven?

There is a lot of confusion about heaven. When some people think of heaven, they think of a sky full of puffy clouds where God and his angels and all the saints of old live. Some even suggest that when people die, they get wings like the angels so they too can fly in the clouds.

But heaven where Jesus reigns is not a place you can get to in an airplane. The Bible tells us that when Jesus left the disciples to return to his Father in heaven, he was lifted up into the clouds. Two angels appeared to the disciples who were watching and said, "Why do you stand looking into heaven? This Jesus, who was taken up from you into heaven, will come in the same way as you saw him go into heaven" (Acts 1:9–11).

As a result of these words some people incorrectly think Jesus is living somewhere in the clouds. The Bible actually uses heaven to talk about three different places:

- Heaven is one name for the sky above the earth (where the disciples were looking when Jesus disappeared).
- Outer space, with all the stars and planets, is also called the "heavens."
- Heaven is also the place where God sits upon his throne—it is where all the angels live and where Christians go when they die. This is where Jesus is now, ruling the world seated at the right hand of the Father (1 Peter 3:21–22).

Do we go to heaven when we die?

The repentant thief on the cross asked Jesus to remember him, and Jesus answered, "Truly, I say to you, today you will be with me in paradise" (Luke 23:43). Paradise is another word for heaven. When the thief who believed in Jesus died, his soul went to be with the Lord in heaven, but his body was buried in a grave and returned to the dust of the earth. The same is true of all Christians. We all grow old and die, and our bodies return to dust; but our soul lives on (Genesis 3:19; 35:18). Our soul is the part of us that loves God and feels happy or sad. Once in heaven with Jesus, we'll join all the Christians who have already died. When Jesus returns to judge the earth and make everything new, we will get new bodies (Philippians 3:20-21). The Bible tells us that Jesus will come with a shout and a trumpet blast and raise our dead bodies (1 Thessalonians 4:13-18), transforming them into glorified bodies (1 Corinthians 15:42-44). Imagine what it will be like to have a body that never grows tired and never gets sick!

On that day, Jesus will judge all evil and send Satan and all his followers, including all the people who refused to believe in Jesus into the lake of fire (Revelation 20:13-15). Once all evil is locked away, God will make the earth brand new (Revelation 21:1-5). There will be no need for the sun, for God's light will light all of heaven (Revelation 21:23; 22:5). God will do away with all sadness, sickness, and pain (Revelation 21:4).

Then all the Christians will praise God. There will be people from every tribe and nation gathered around the throne to praise God (Revelation 7:9-10). Like in the Garden of Eden, God will plant the tree of life (Revelation 22:1-2). We will join Jesus in ruling the earth (Revelation 2:26; 3:21) and even judge angels (1 Corinthians 6:3).

What will the new heavens be like?

Imagine what it will be like hiking through the new earth in our brand new bodies. God will restore peace to the earth so that the wolf will not attack the lamb (Isaiah 11:6-9). We'll get to talk to people like Moses and ask him, "What was it like to walk through the Red Sea on dry ground?" But best of all, we will get to walk with Jesus and see him face-to-face (1 Corinthians 13:12).

So you see, God made his children for heaven and he is working to bring us all home where we will praise and glorify God and enjoy him forever (Isaiah 43:5-7).

Who can go to heaven?

Anyone who trusts in Jesus and asks forgiveness for their sins! Jesus paid for your sins when he died on the cross. It doesn't matter how bad you have been or how mean, when you ask Jesus to forgive you for your sins and be in charge of your life, you are forgiven. Now you are ready for heaven! Now you are also ready to tell others the good news that they can go to heaven too—all they have to do is trust Jesus and ask for forgiveness too.

Discussion Questions

- What did you learn about heaven from this story?

- Everyone who trusts in the Lord will be saved and go to heaven. What happens to those who reject Jesus and refuse to believe?

- What do you think it will be like to meet Jesus and see him face to face?

- What do you think it will be like to join God's heavenly family and meet all the famous Bible characters who believed in God? Whom would you want to meet? What would you ask them?

This book is dedicated to
Randy Alcorn,
author and founder of Eternal Perspective Ministries.

Randy's depiction of heaven through his writing has shaped my view of eternity, and that of millions of others all across the globe and has increased our longing for our Savior's return.

New Growth Press, Greensboro, NC 27404
Text Copyright © 2021 by Marty Machowski
Illustration Copyright © 2021 by Trish Mahoney

All rights reserved. No part of this publication may be reproduced, stored in a retrieval system, or transmitted in any form by any means, electronic, mechanical, photocopy, recording, or otherwise, without the prior permission of the publisher, except as provided by USA copyright law.

Scripture quotations are from The ESV® Bible (The Holy Bible, English Standard Version®), copyright © 2001 by Crossway, a publishing ministry of Good News Publishers. Used by permission. All rights reserved.

Art and Design: Trish Mahoney

ISBN: 978-1-64507-071-9

Library of Congress Cataloging-in-Publication Data

Names: Machowski, Martin, 1963- author. | Mahoney, Trish, illustrator.
Title: God made me for heaven : helping children live for an eternity with Jesus / by Marty Machowski ; illustrated by Trish Mahoney.
Description: Greensboro, NC : New Growth Press, 2021. | Series: God made me series | Audience: Ages 4-8 | Summary: "Marty Machowski shares deep theological truths about heaven through a creative story"-- Provided by publisher.
Identifiers: LCCN 2020047154 | ISBN 9781645070719 (hardback)
Subjects: LCSH: Heaven--Christianity--Juvenile literature. | Christian education of children.
Classification: LCC BT849 .M33 2021 | DDC 236/.24--dc23
LC record available at https://lccn.loc.gov/2020047154

Printed in Canada
28 27 26 25 24 23 22 21   1 2 3 4 5